Living Frugally

A Guide to Survival

I0450561

Prepping and Survival Series

M. Usman

Mendon Cottage Books

JD-Biz Publishing

Disclaimer

The information is this book is provided for informational purposes only. It is not intended to be used and medical advice or a substitute for proper medical treatment by a qualified health care provider. The information is believed to be accurate as presented based on research by the author.

The contents have not been evaluated by the U.S. Food and Drug Administration or any other Government or Health Organization and the contents in this book are not to be used to treat cure or prevent disease.

The author or publisher is not responsible for the use or safety of any diet, procedure or treatment mentioned in this book. The author or publisher is not responsible for errors or omissions that may exist.

Warning

The Book is for informational purposes only and before taking on any diet, treatment or medical procedure, it is recommended to consult with your primary health care provider.

Our books are available at

1. Amazon.com
2. Barnes and Noble
3. Itunes
4. Kobo
5. Smashwords
6. Google Play Books

Table of Contents

Introduction 4

Chapter 1 - The Myth of Frugality 5

Chapter 2 - Why live frugally? 7

Chapter 3 - Lessons in frugality 8

Fine tuning your grocery shopping 10

    Rules for grocery shopping 10

Frugal eating 12

Frugal activities 14

    Your car 14

    Shelter 14

    Fashion clothing and accessories 15

    Offline and online buying 15

    Fun and recreation 16

    Your health and fitness 16

    Other frugal ways 17

The warm and cold of it 20

    The warms 20

    The colds 20

Conclusion 22

Author Bio 23

Publisher 34

Introduction

Living frugally comes naturally to some. For others, it is a task that has be thought through, each and every day. Every person has a different reason for wanting to change his or her lifestyle. Some want to save more money, while others have had a financial crisis, and a few just want to challenge their selves. Throughout this book, we will cover what it means to be frugal, as well as, some ways to help you along your journey.

The definition of frugal says a person who is economical or thrifty, and implies that a frugal person is extra careful of their use of everyday resources. We will discuss this more in the coming chapters, so get ready to transform your lifestyle!

Chapter 1 - The Myth of Frugality

Just like many people, you probably think that frugal living is cheap and stingy. Surprisingly, this is just a myth. People who live frugally are more interested in leading a debt-free, stress-free life. They understand their priorities quite well and spend their money based on a rational budget.

Another common myth is that people who are frugal do not have a better choice. Although, there are some of us who have to economize, for others it is just a choice. They usually put a value to all the time, money, labor and other resources they use to survive. Instead of buying an item just because it is trendy, frugal folks will leave it or look for a high quality replacement.

Enemies of frugality normally view it as extreme self denial and sacrifice. This is not true. Though economizing might be viewed as useless self denial, physically, those who like it have an emotional gain. They have mastered the art of living within their means. They have no debt, and this translates to a worry-free way of life. This is unlike someone who buys things on impulse, regardless of whether they have similar items or money to spend.

There is a myth that frugality is impractical in modern times. In the past few decades families were okay with the rural lifestyle, which was simple, reserved, and self-sufficient. Today people have moved to the city where class and elegance matters. Living frugally in the modern times is thus a personal decision, driven by the desire to avoid extravagance while adopting a saving habit. So saying that leading a frugal life in the modern times is impossible is just a myth. Countless frugal persons exist today.

There are some of you who think that frugality has no place for fashion and trend. This, again, is just a myth. Many frugal individuals are sincerely stylish and approachable. However, they have their own definition of being fashionable and stylish. Instead of buying a garment because everybody wants it, frugal shoppers look for a quality design, a good fit, a durable fabric and durable stitching. Their other trick is to compare prices to see if there are shopkeepers who are willing to offer a discount.

Some of you feel that frugality is too hard and demanding. This may be true, particularly if you are not used to living with a number of financial limits. As you continue, however, frugality will get easier and more like your second nature. It is the fact that you will stop irrational spending and impulse buying that will make frugality difficult at first.

Making a choice to live frugally from now on is yours. Just see it as the main answer to living in debt, living beyond your means, and living with constant stress.

Chapter 2 - Why live frugally?

Why live frugally when you have enough to spend? First, it is because frugal living can allow you to spend less money than you earn so that you can save, pay a debt, or start an investment project.

Another simple reason is that the less money you spend, the less you have to earn. Consequently you can stop being a workaholic now or even choose to work harder now, so as to retire early and enjoy life.

Living frugally can let you take short-term breaks from work as well. Investing and saving culture, will guarantee enough bucks to spend when you are on temporary retirements. When you take a break you can also enjoy free moments with your family, do fun things, exercise, and simply spend your leisure as you please.

Living within your means can truly be a treasure if you were to get fired from your job or if your business were to collapse in the future. Your ongoing investments and savings can help you start all over again.

But, if you cannot sacrifice now just to buy useless things that will depreciate in value with time, you are likely to suffer should your current source of money deteriorate or disappear in future.

If you eat whole healthy food now, instead of cheap, regular junk, you might age gracefully, and perhaps escape expensive degenerative diseases in future.

There are many other reasons for living frugally, including a personal choice to be modest.

Chapter 3 - Lessons in frugality

Are you a parent? If so, your kids need frugal living lessons from you. If you can take the time to teach them how to ride a bicycle, dress themselves, use a potty, and other small things, why can you not give them financial lessons as well?

Children observe grown ups in order to learn. So if you live beyond your means and want to teach your child how to live within its means, you will fail miserably. You must first learn to live frugally so as to pass the same skill effectively to a child.

There is another warning too: do not go overboard with your frugal lessons. It can send an unintended message to a child. Do not force your kid to learn frugality; use practical money saving examples instead. By so doing you will allow your baby to reason and see the point.

First you want to set a money saving goal for your child. You may suggest saving up for a vacation to a place that your child likes. For instance, you could save up for a trip to Disneyland instead of buying something at the store that your kid already has.

Instead of frequently taking your kids to a theater to watch a movie, you can buy them a new, fifteen dollar DVD each month. Theaters are too expensive for families, as they will need some snacks and drinks. On the other hand, buying a DVD and watching it at home for free is a great way to save money.

Books are not only needed by children, but also adults. So it would make sense to get a library card that would allow all of you to check out DVDs and books from the library. This can be cheaper than buying new books, even if you might be put on the waiting list.

Children cannot relate with money and time spent to earn it. So for them to understand the value for money you should teach them how to compare prices of different items when shopping. They will see for themselves how taking the time to compare prices can save their money. Then, they will realize that the more you save the less you need to work and that the more you spend the harder you must work to recover your money.

Kids are obviously good at impulse buying. They want to have everything they consider beautiful and humorous, even if they have a similar item at home. It is very imperative to teach your children how to buy something because it is really necessary. Buying items just because they are all the rage, might save them fifty percent.

But, if they will buy and not use that item, it would have been easier to save one hundred percent by not ordering it at all. Children may hesitate first because it means denying themselves something they want, but sooner than later they will accept this frugal lesson. They will even remind each other that they need to save one hundred percent on wants rather than needs.

The concept of frugality should not only be viewed in terms of money. The time you spend teaching your kids how to be responsible with finances will pay off much later in life. To instill discipline in saving, you should teach kids that money is earned. This frugal lesson can be taught easily by assigning responsibilities, and if completed nicely, the child is paid. By so doing you will raise a child that is not only independent but also cooperative.

Fine tuning your grocery shopping

There are families that buy excess food only to throw out up to twenty percent of it every week. Throwing away food is just not right, because there are people who go hungry for several days in a lot of countries.

The main cause of this is either overestimating the food you would eat at home each week or being undisciplined about eating outside. Having raw groceries around is fine if you can spare time to cook it. On the other hand, buying too much is pointless if you aren't going to cook it.

Items that go bad after a few months, such as butter, cheese, oil, balsamic vinegar and the like, should be bought in smaller quantities of great quality. It is not frugal to buy these items in bulk unless they have good quality.

Do you like spices? Note that some species will go stale after a year of use and this will cause them to lose their flavor. Leave out spices that your family does not like, as it will only consume shelf space and go to waste later on.

Rules for grocery shopping

Impulse buying is not recommended if you want your kitchen to be economical. With the following fool-proof rules you can adopt a cheap, more efficient, and less wasteful standard of living with reference to grocery shopping.

- Keep a list of items that you have depleted to avoid impulse buying.

- Buy some items in smaller amounts in their freshest form.

- Clean the bottles or containers you use to keep some food stuffs so you can know what you need to replace when you go shopping.

- Schedule your shopping exercise based on the nature of groceries you use and your best stores. For instance, you could purchase fruits and vegetables once or twice a week. In addition, you could purchase non-perishable groceries like cereals or canned goods once a month.

As soon as you start frugal grocery shopping you will no longer throw away food. Your food store and fridge will become orderly as well. What's more, are your home cooked meals will forever be delicious because your groceries will be fresh. Above all you will save money, as you will regulate the amount of food that is bought and eaten.

Frugal eating

How much do you spend on food? Many people, especially those who have families, spend lots of money on food and drinks. If you want to start eating frugally, read our suggestions as shown below:

Plan and cook ahead – Many mothers are busy all through the week. If you are busy as well, plan a whole week's shopping and cook ahead to avoid wasting money in expensive restaurants. When you feel too tired to prepare meals after work you can just warm your frozen meals.

Avoid eating out a lot - An average individual is estimated to spend about two thousand dollars a year in restaurants. This is because restaurants sell expensive fast food that is not even healthy. It is easier to buy fresh groceries and prepare meals at home. If you must eat out, be sure to save money. For instance, if you have many children, they could share one plate of food.

Have you ordered from restaurants' kids menu recently? Meals are big and smaller children do not eat as much as we adults do. Another way to reduce your restaurant budget is to hunt for coupons on the internet. You may follow the restaurants you like on Twitter or Facebook. One day in the future you might just be reward with a coupon.

Meat is expensive – Instead of eating meat daily or often, you can try a vegetarian lifestyle once in a while. There are many vegetarian recipes you can easily make at home and they can be found online. Eventually, you will be healthier than a person who eats meat daily and you will definitely save a lot of money. If you have to buy chicken, pick a whole one most of the times instead of boneless and skinless chicken parts that are more expensive.

Save money on seafood - Fresh seafood is very expensive. Frozen fish can be a good alternative, as it is forty percent cheaper than seafood sold at the counter. That's roughly three-point-two dollars cheaper per pound of cod fillet. Per year you could save over $100 if you cook fish only once a week.

Plan grocery shopping – For most families groceries are a major expenditure. With the simple routines mentioned above you could save a lot of money on groceries. The most important thing is to order just what you need.

Cook your lunch – According to a past survey, two thirds of employees spend thirty-seven dollars every week on lunch. In order to spend half of this amount you should cook your own meals. It is possible to save over $900 in the long run if you get into the habit of carrying your own lunch.

Do not always take soft drinks – According to nutritionists, soft drinks like sodas contain "empty" calories that won't build your health. They should not always be taken when families go out. Your family can take pure, clean water instead. Approximately one hundred dollars could be saved per year.

Grow your own herbs and vegetables – Container farming is becoming rampant in the cities nowadays. Herbs and vegetables like tomatoes, green leafy vegetables, and even some fruits, do well in container gardens. What if you grow your own instead of paying hefty amounts each time? There is enough information on container gardening on the internet.

Frugal activities

The cost of living has definitely gone up nowadays. There are countless people who just cannot survive without cutting back their current expenses. In other words, some of us are finding frugal living irresistible. There are many activities that you can engage in to live frugally. They are described as shown below.

Your car

Although this is the most useful asset you can have, a car can be too expensive to handle if you are not organized. The more cars you own the more your monthly expenditures will increase. If it is possible for all family members to use one car, you will save a lot on gas and other maintenance costs in the long run.

You can also save a lot of money on gas if you drive a smaller auto. If you are not using a car for business, then you do not need a big, high maintenance vehicle. What if you get a car repair manual online to help you assess your auto's problems? This will save you a lot of money as you will stop paying your mechanic even when your car has a small mechanical fault.

An automatic device sold online is meant to help motorists reduce their gas bill by a 1/3 each year. It is priced at $100 on a site like automatic.com. To avoid causing careless accidents on the road and paying about ten percent more on your auto insurance, you could try a defensive driving course. It will take only about four hours of your time on the internet.

Did you know that some insurers offer discounts for low-mileage autos? These are autos that are driven fewer than seven thousand five hundred to fifteen thousand miles per annum. You could get a ten percent discount and roughly save up to seventy-nine dollars per annum. What if you use the cheaper public transport buses a few times a week? Buses are definitely cheaper than personal vehicles, although they operate on their own terms. Suppose you travel in a single car with friends or relatives who live near you. There is a possibility of pocketing more savings.

Shelter

This is obviously a basic need that you cannot do without. Even so, you have a choice with regard to the cost of housing. The first sacrifice you must make is living in a smaller house, even if you can afford a bigger one. A small comfortable house with adequate space for everyone is okay. As you will find out, living in a small house will save you thousands each year.

In order to increase your living space in a small house, you could auction your clutter on eBay. If you do your math carefully and correctly you might find that renting is cheaper than buying. Additionally, a used house that could do with a little remodeling may suit your financial circumstances better than a new house. Just take the time to weigh and compare your choices regarding housing.

Fashion clothing and accessories

Besides groceries, families waste a lot of money on fashion apparel and accessories. The problem with some people is that they want to buy every new designer item they see on the runways. If you often borrow a payday loan to buy clothes, shoes, and bags, you should change this habit as it can land you in debt. Instead you should mix and match your clothes to look like you have a variety. Buying casual and formal fashion items is important though, as you will need them at different times.

Adopting a minimalist wardrobe is just fine as well, if it can work for you. It is also imperative to buy new clothes only when they are really necessary. As you do, take the time to locate bargain clothing stores. Thrift stores might have good clothes, even if they are second class. Online clothes shopping can be cheaper too, because you can get a chance to compare prices offered by different stores.

To avoid going back to the shops too soon, you should maintain and care for your clothes. For instance, you want to wash your clothing after wearing them more than once, unless they are very dirty. You can smell your clothes before putting them on again. Recycling outer clothes like jackets and sweaters can reduce wear and tear and save detergents, energy, and water.

During summer there is enough sun to dry your garments. With a few clotheslines you can begin to dry clothes outdoors and save electricity that dryers use. Sun-dried clothes smell fresh and last longer too. You will only use a little amount of energy to hang them up on the line.

Offline and online buying

Although shopping online is fun, some people will overindulge and regret it later on. It is very easy to do impulse purchases online because of the ease of shopping with a credit card. What's more, online shoppers just need a mouse click to open a new shop or store. This is unlike those who shop offline as they are forced to walk or drive to the stores.

If you want to stop online impulse buying you have to cancel your credit card first. This will control your addiction with reference to buying everything that attracts your eyes. If you cannot keep your feet out of the malls, then you have a problem to solve. Perhaps you should avoid your triggers, such as driving to a shopping complex or taking your equally obsessed friends to a department store. They might influence you and make you spend money that would have been saved.

Then, when visiting a mall for some shopping you should always carry a list of things you really need to avoid ordering things just for fun. Unnecessary items could add up fast making you overspend. If you cannot use your credit card responsibly, just skip it. Haven't you heard of people who have struggled with credit card debt? Debt starts when one monthly bill is omitted either partly or fully. Perhaps you have found yourself misusing your credit card and this is really a bad idea. Soon you might find yourself among the Americans who owe over $8,500 in credit card debt.

With online shopping, it is necessary to cancel some magazine, newspaper, and newsletter subscriptions in favor of free news websites. They even offer free DVDs. If there are some paid subscriptions you can replace with free ones, just do it to save money. Books consume a lot of money when being bought. If you love reading, perhaps you can visit your local library a few times a month to check out the books you might like. There are also some libraries that offer valuable information on DVDs.

Fun and recreation

People spend a lot of cash on entertainment, which is fine. However, in this day and age everyone wants to live frugally or at least save some money. If you love entertainment you can find free options. Going out to the bar, malls, theaters, hotels, parks, and other paid places to have fun will be very expensive in the long run. There are cheaper and more enjoyable means of having fun along with your family. Instead of renting a car you could drive yours unless you want to fly out of your state.

It will even be cheaper if you could just get in the bus or train. When you must fly away for a holiday, make sure that you book your tickets in advance. Last minute tickets can be expensive, because of lack of discount deals. In addition, look for an accommodation that you can afford in the city you are visiting. The internet is full of trustworthy travel agencies that you can seek information from. Note that travelling away to enjoy life is recommended, but not when you have piles of debt.

Your health and fitness

Many modern people are very interested in losing weight and maintaining good health and fitness. If you have a gym membership that you are struggling to keep, just hold it. Putting your gym membership on hold is usually cheaper monthly than maintaining a full service monthly membership. During summer you could easily stop gym activity and start biking, hiking, swimming, scuba diving, mountaineering, and so on.

Many people have lost weight and gotten their shape back via biking. What if you begin to commute to work by your bike? It will not only keep your body fit but will also save a lot of your money. Walking to all the nearest places you want to go to is a simpler way to maintain a healthy weight. It will also save your gas and refresh your mind.

Smoking is an unhealthy habit that puts your future at risk. Although it seems too difficult to quit now, you can do it. There are many people we all know that used to be chain smokers and they have been clean for years now. You will not only stop buying cigarettes, but also chewing gums, soda, or beer. There are, of course, the long-term costs associated with smoking cigarettes, including lung cancer.

If you take beer or alcohol you should also moderate use or stop for the sake of your health and saving money. A few of you drink one or more bottles a day, not to mention buying some for friends. It would be wiser to moderate your drinking so as to take beer during an occasional party or when with your buddies. This will mean cutting nights with your pals as they will influence you to drink or smoke.

White sugar, desserts, and sweets are delicious, but they add useless calories to your system. They make you gain weight and develop teeth decay problems. You also want to reduce use of sodas, juices (not fresh fruit and vegetable juices), coffee, and tea. In their place you can take pure water.

Other frugal ways

DIY method - When you choose Do-It-Yourself instead of buying a repair service you can save lots of cash in the long-term. For instance, you can repair your kitchen sink pipes instead of calling a plumber. Also you can mow your lawn or trim your hedge instead of paying someone to do it. Besides repairing, you can make some things from the scratch such as bookshelves, rugs, outdoor benches, chicken coops, and decks, among other things. The internet has plans for making different things. Making an item yourself will always be cheaper. There are some of us who will even shave our own hair with an electric clipper.

Check your cell phone bill - Are you spending too much on communication? A cell phone, unless used for business, should not consume a lot of money. A phone call to just joke with your friends is really just a waste of money. Think about your own cell phone monthly bill and see if it can do with a cut down. If you want to make international calls you can use Skype to connect to anybody on earth. It will only cost you about $4 monthly to connect to a UK landline, for instance, and you will take for four hundred minutes. Cell phone bill is roughly $10 a month, meaning that you can save up to seventy-two dollars using Skype.

Save energy - To save energy you should consider all the appliances that use electricity or gas in your house. Are there some appliances that consume too much unnecessary energy and are there alternatives? Wind turbines and solar panels are alternative sources of electric energy and there is a lot of information on the internet on how they should be installed.

Light bulbs could also consume needless energy if not selected carefully. Power savers are available. Also, you can open windows rather than turn on your lights during the day.

To save cooking gas, as its price has been rising uncontrollably, you must choose your pans carefully. Pans that have dull surfaces, wider bottoms and metallic surfaces can help you save on gas. Also, you want to ensure that your cooker has a blue to colorless flame. A yellow flame is an indication that the energy within the burner is poorly harnessed.

Save water - In order to reduce your water bill annually, you can take shorter showers, meaning you are going to shave a few minutes off the shower. Doing this could easily save up to nineteen dollars annually. You can have a grey water recycling system built to make further use of bathroom and sink water. It can be used in your flower garden, toilet and other places.

Insurance – You could cut your insurance bill by as much as twenty percent, if you bundle your homeowners and car insurance together. When both insurance covers are separate you can spend up to 1,700 dollars per annum. If you reduce this by twenty percent it means you will save about three hundred and forty dollars a year.

Home made cleaners – There are blogs that educate people on making soaps and other cleaners at home. If you learn to make these soaps you can save up to forty dollars per year.

Frugal Christmas – Families spend a lot of money during Christmas here in the US. Some will literally throw away their hard earned money on expensive gifts, only to come down with nothing to spend in January. There are cheaper ways to celebrate Christmas without having to overuse.

The most important thing is to plan ahead of Christmas so that by the time it come you have a bunch of fun things you can afford to do and see. The same should apply when celebrating birthdays and other family events.

Reduce your errands – Running errands is a must, but you can batch some so you do not have to run a one errand each day. Do all of them together to save time and money. Paying most of your bills online can get rid of errands.

Earn extra from home – This is not so much on saving money as earning it. Instead of taking another job outside, you could telecommute in order to save money on gas, dinner, and other things. There are people who end up telecommuting full time. It is your choice. Another way to earn cash easily is to auction your things on eBay or Amazon.

The warm and cold of it

It takes impulse buyers a long time to realize that they are following a path that will eventually lead to destruction. Adopting a frugal lifestyle has its warms and colds. The warms (advantages) are definitely more than the colds (disadvantages). For this reason, many people are learning to be frugal despite the few challenges they must face prior to getting used to it.

The warms

One of the advantages to living frugally is obviously to save money. Who doesn't need to save money in this day and age? The cost of living is escalating quickly and people must save while looking for new ways to make money. Besides saving up money, frugality beats therapy for anxiety, depression, and stress. Frugal people are usually in control of their own money.

They are disciplined enough to live with only what they can afford now. This increases their feelings of gratitude and contentment while reducing the stress associated with money. They find it easier and healthier to eliminate the lifestyle that is causing anxiety than to sustain it with borrowed money. When one is not at the mercy of debt collectors, they can avoid worrying about making it to the next paycheck.

Because they have built their savings, they can take temporary leaves, change jobs, start a business, retire early, work in old age, and do whatever they see fit for their lives. Frugality eliminates the feeling of being trapped in debt and unending emotional problems. Truly frugal people are survivors; if they cannot afford it they can learn how to make it.

The colds

Frugality has its own disadvantages. First it is difficult, especially when a person does not know how to put limits to their spending. It takes serious choices and sacrifice to embrace true frugality. Frugal people are risk averse and therefore lose out in the possibility of getting higher returns on investment. They are used to doing things in moderation, meaning that they invest smaller amounts until they get a reward.

Risk takers will, on the other hand, invest abundantly without worrying about losing everything. Frugal folks fix their eye on expenses rather than their income. This is obviously a good financial management tip, but it needs a little moderation not to cause negative consequences. When cutting costs becomes the focal point, the bread winner might get comfortable with just earning less because it is enough for the family. This may lead to less income in retirement time.

Conclusion

Throughout this book, we have established what it takes for you to transform your life to living frugally. There are many perks and only a few disadvantages, as we have explained. No one can change overnight, and it will take hard work and lots of discipline, but the results will make it worthwhile.

I hope this book helped to shed some light on a new way of living for you and your family.

Author Bio

Muhammad Usman is a distinguished medical graduate of Allama Iqbal medical college (AIMC). He is a professional writer who has been in the field for more than 4 years. During this time he has produced 10,000+ articles, blogs, and eBooks on various niches related to diseases, health, fitness, nutrition, and well-being. He is a regular contributor to several journals related to medicine and surgery. He is the editor of several journals and newspapers.

Check out some of the other JD-Biz Publishing books

Gardening Series on Amazon

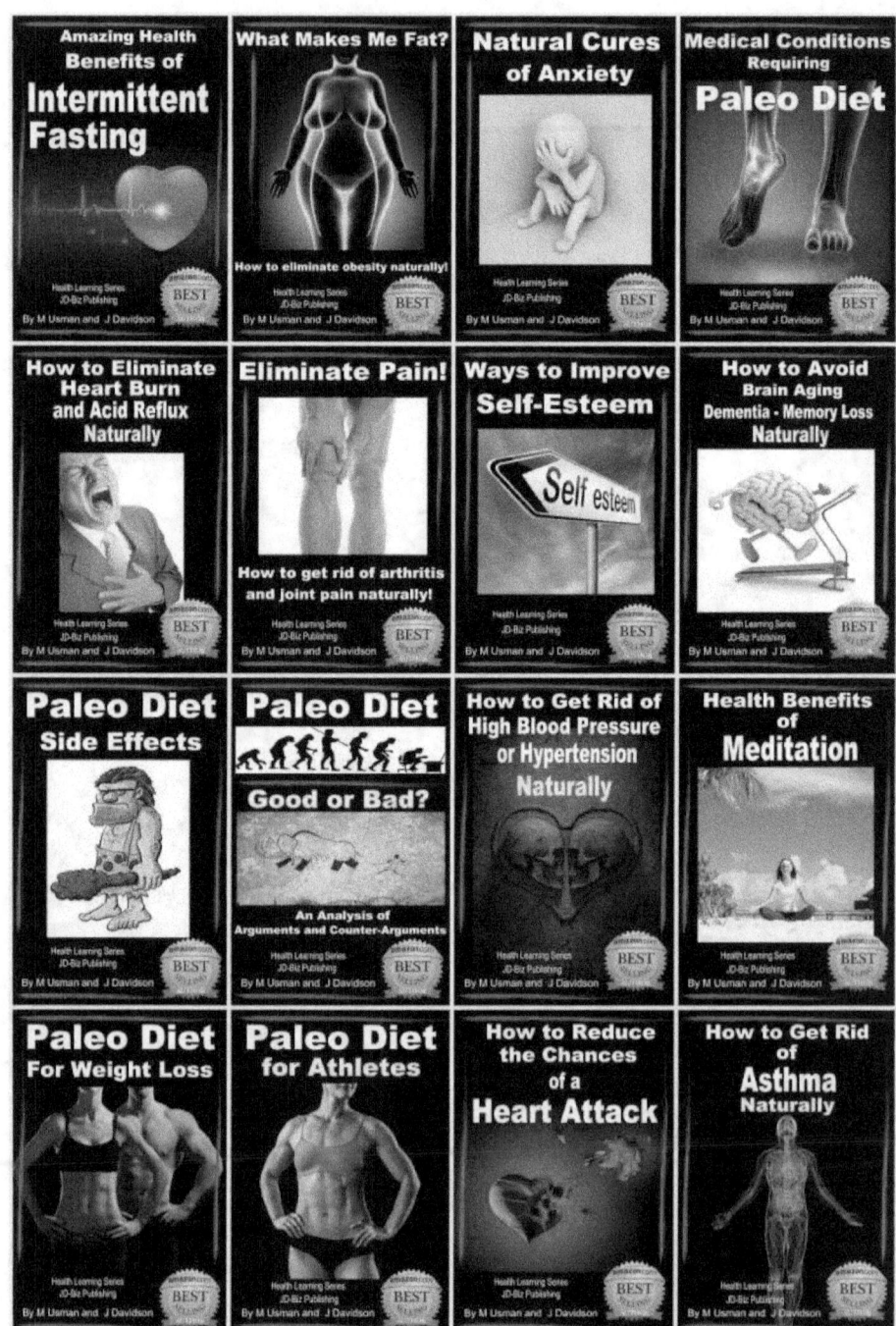

Learn To Draw Series

How to Build and Plan Books

Entrepreneur Book Series

Our books are available at

1. Amazon.com

2. Barnes and Noble

3. Itunes

4. Kobo

5. Smashwords

6. Google Play Books

Publisher

JD-Biz Corp

P O Box 374

Mendon, Utah 84325

http://www.jd-biz.com/

Mendon Cottage Books

P O Box 374, Mendon Utah 84325